MUSIC FROM THE MOTION PICTURE
ARRANGED FOR PIANO SOLO
COMPOSED BY PHILIP GLA

MERYL STREEP

JULIANNE MOORE

NICOLE KIDMAN

{THE}

HOURS

PARAMOUNT PICTURES and MIRAMAX FILMS PRESENT A SCOTT RUDIN/ROBERT FOX PRODUCTION
MERYL STREEP   JULIANNE MOORE   NICOLE KIDMAN
"THE HOURS" ED HARRIS TONI COLLETTE CLAIRE DANES JEFF DANIELS STEPHEN DILLANE
ALLISON JANNEY JOHN C. REILLY MIRANDA RICHARDSON MUSIC BY PHILIP GLASS COSTUME DESIGNER ANN ROTH FILM EDITOR PETER BOYLE
PRODUCTION DESIGNER MARIA DJURKOVIC DIRECTOR OF PHOTOGRAPHY SEAMUS McGARVEY, BSC EXECUTIVE PRODUCER MARK HUFFAM BASED UPON THE NOVEL BY MICHAEL CUNNINGHAM
MIRAMAX FILMS PG-13 PARENTS STRONGLY CAUTIONED Some Material May Be Inappropriate for Children Under 13 SCREENPLAY BY DAVID HARE PRODUCED BY SCOTT RUDIN ROBERT FOX DIRECTED BY STEPHEN DALDRY Paramount 90th ANNIVERSARY

READ THE NOVEL FROM PICADOR USA   FOR MATURE THEMATIC ELEMENTS, SOME DISTURBING IMAGES & BRIEF LANGUAGE   DOLBY DIGITAL IN SELECTED THEATRES   READ THE SCREENPLAY FROM TALK MIRAMAX BOOKS   TheHoursMovie.com   TM BY PARAMOUNT PICTURES. COPYRIGHT © 2002 BY PARAMOUNT PICTURES AND MIRAMAX FILM CORP. ALL RIGHTS RESERVED.   SOUNDTRACK ALBUM AVAILABLE ON NONESUCH RECORDS

WISE PUBLICATIONS
LONDON / NEW YORK / PARIS / SYDNEY / COPENHAGEN / BERLIN / MADRID / TOKYO

Published by:
Wise Publications
8-9 Frith Street, London, W1D 3JB.

Exclusive distributors:
Music Sales Limited
Newmarket Road, Bury St Edmunds, Suffolk, IP33 3YB, England.

Music Sales Pty Limited
120 Rothschild Avenue, Rosebery, NSW 2018, Australia.

Order No. AM977383
ISBN 1-84449-061-0
This book © Copyright 2003 Wise Publications.

Music engraved by Camden Music.
Edited by Christopher Hussey.
Printed in the United Kingdom.

Your Guarantee of Quality:
As publishers, we strive to produce every book to the highest commercial standards.
This book has been freshly engraved and avoids awkward page turns making playing from it a real pleasure.
Particular care has been given to specifying acid-free, neutral-sized paper made from
pulps which have not been elemental chlorine bleached.
The pulp is from farmed sustainable forests and was produced with special regard for the environment.
Throughout, the printing and binding have been planned to ensure a sturdy,
attractive publication which should give years of enjoyment.
If your copy fails to meet our high standards, please inform us and we will gladly replace it.

www.musicsales.com

The Poet Acts

COMPOSED BY PHILIP GLASS
ARRANGED BY MICHAEL RIESMAN AND NICO MÜHLY

Morning Passages

COMPOSED BY PHILIP GLASS
ARRANGED BY MICHAEL RIESMAN AND NICO MÜHLY

Something She Has To Do

COMPOSED BY PHILIP GLASS
ARRANGED BY MICHAEL RIESMAN AND NICO MÜHLY

I'm Going To Make A Cake

COMPOSED BY PHILIP GLASS
ARRANGED BY MICHAEL RIESMAN AND NICO MÜHLY

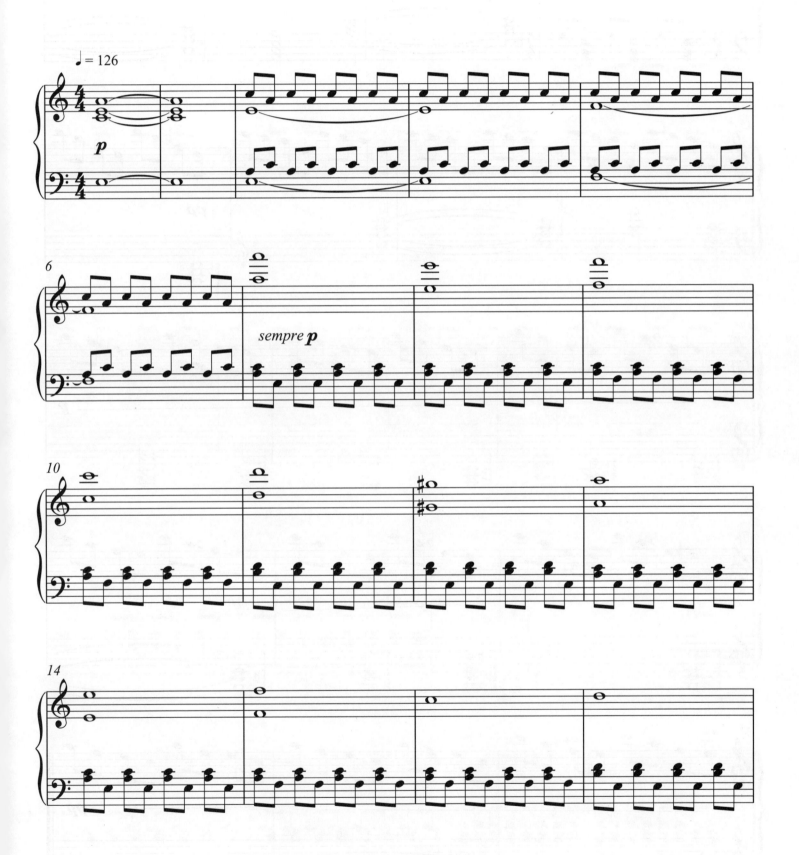

An Unwelcome Friend

COMPOSED BY PHILIP GLASS
ARRANGED BY MICHAEL RIESMAN AND NICO MÜHLY

Dead Things

COMPOSED BY PHILIP GLASS
ARRANGED BY MICHAEL RIESMAN AND NICO MÜHLY

Why Does Someone Have To Die?

COMPOSED BY PHILIP GLASS
ARRANGED BY MICHAEL RIESMAN AND NICO MÜHLY

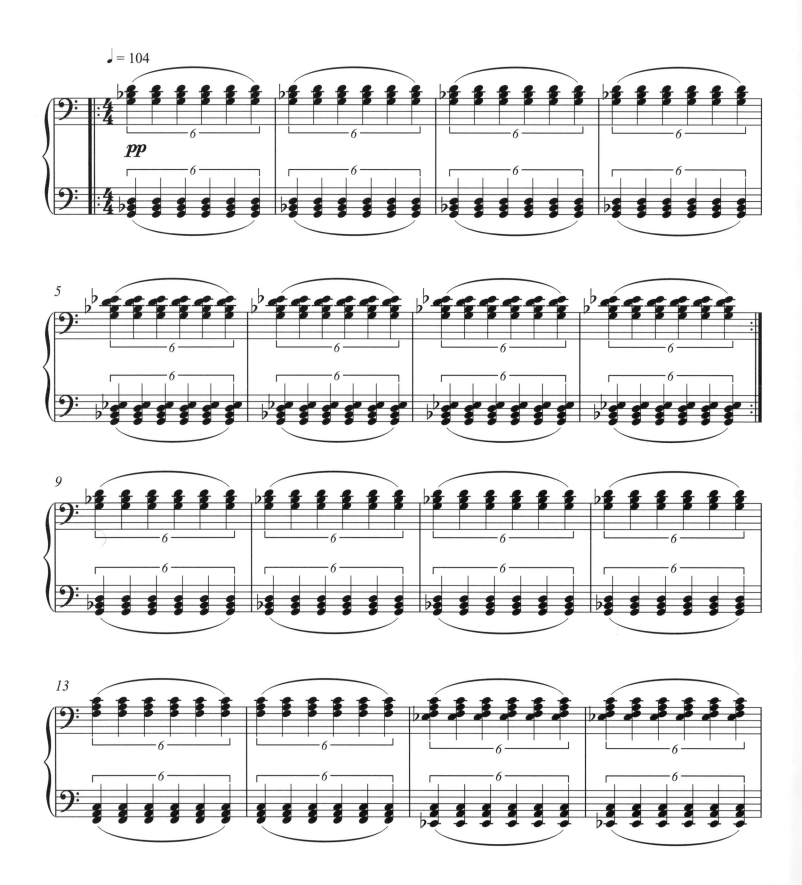

Tearing Herself Away

COMPOSED BY PHILIP GLASS
ARRANGED BY MICHAEL RIESMAN AND NICO MÜHLY

Escape!

COMPOSED BY PHILIP GLASS
ARRANGED BY MICHAEL RIESMAN AND NICO MÜHLY

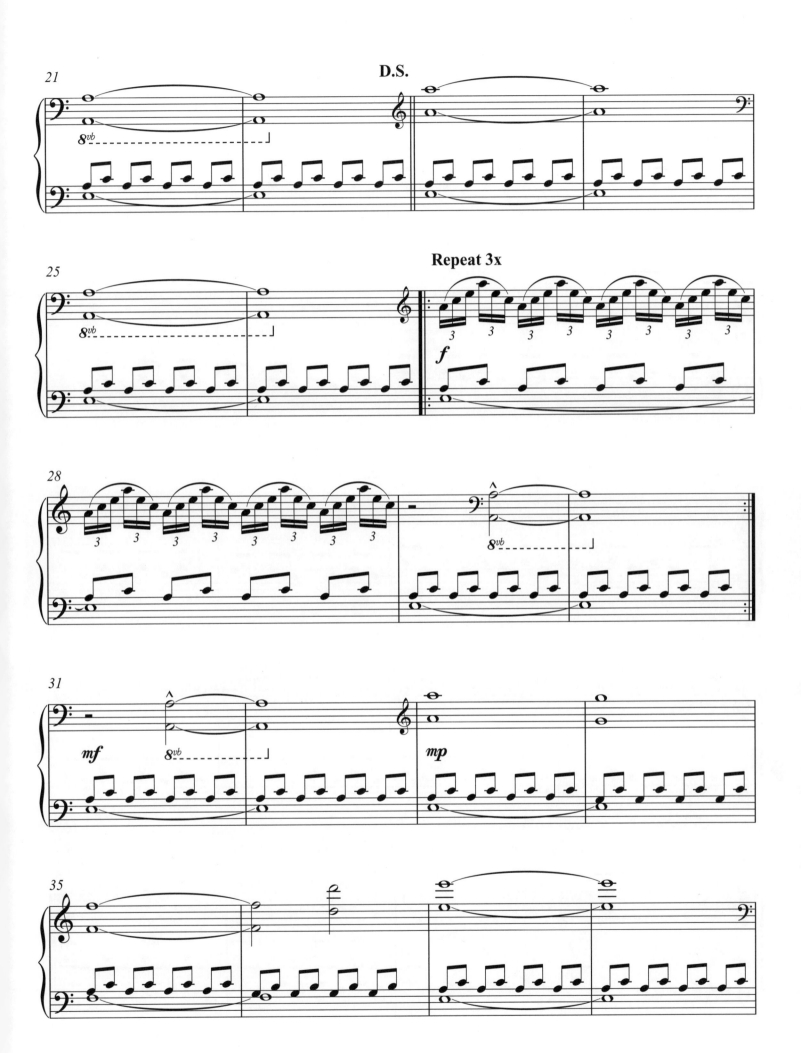

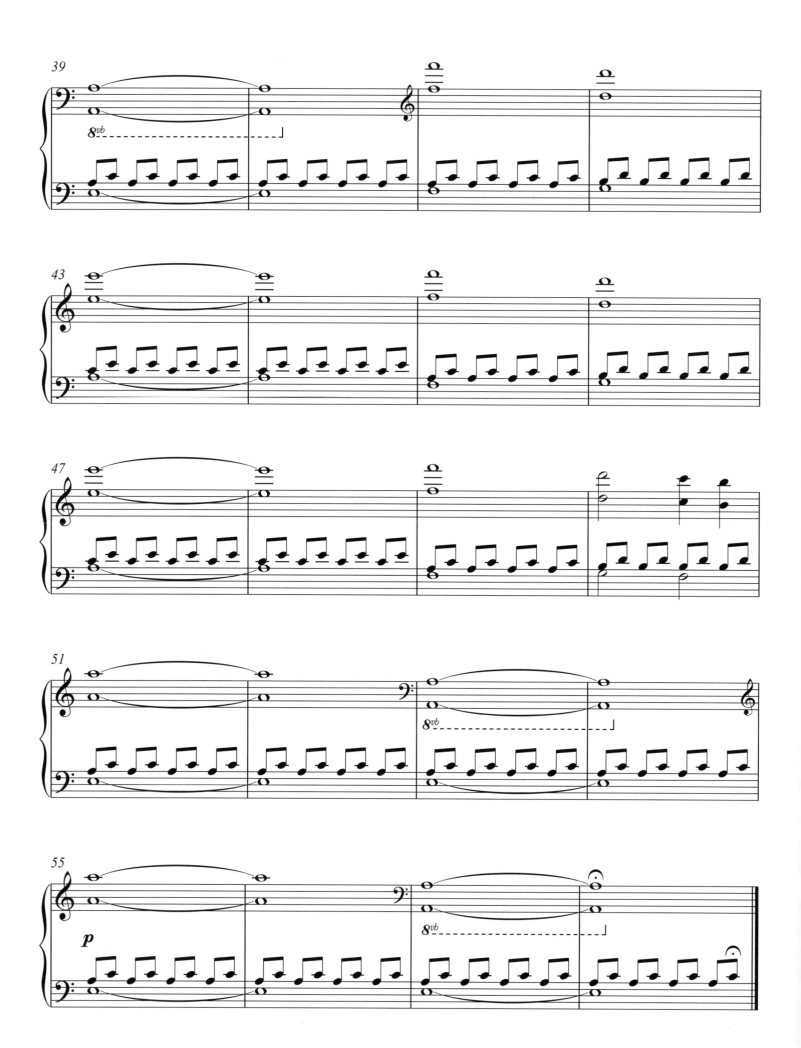

Choosing Life

COMPOSED BY PHILIP GLASS
ARRANGED BY MICHAEL RIESMAN AND NICO MÜHLY

The Hours

COMPOSED BY PHILIP GLASS
ARRANGED BY MICHAEL RIESMAN AND NICO MÜHLY